LIVING IN SPIN

HOW MEDIA GURUS AND PR CZARS OPEN OUR WALLETS AND SCRAMBLE OUR LOGIC

BY NEAL LARSON
OF THE NEAL LARSON SHOW
WITH REBECCA H. ADAMS, MD

Living in Spin.
Published by Neven Media.
Cover design by Ethan Russon
Interior design by Emily Russon
Copyright © 2016 by Neal Larson and Rebecca Adams.

ISBN-13: 978-1523603855
IBN-10: 1523603852

ABOUT THE AUTHORS

NEAL LARSON

Neal Larson is the host of The Neal Larson Show, which airs regionally across Idaho and Wyoming. An Associated Press award-winning newspaper columnist, he holds a BA from Idaho State University in Media Studies and Political Science. He also serves as public address announcer for Idaho State University Athletics. Neal can be reached online at www. NealLarson.com. Neal and his wife, Esther, are happily married with five children and live in Idaho Falls, Idaho.

DR. REBECCA ADAMS

Dr. Rebecca Adams is a Board Certified Family Medicine physician with a passion for writing and special interest in politics, history, marketing, and psychology. She and her husband, also a physician, have three sons and a small farm in Idaho.

TABLE OF CONTENTS

INTRODUCTION

I'm guilty.

But most of you probably are, too. Quite often I walk to the back of the convenience store, open the beverage cooler and grab a nice cold bottle of...water. This, despite the fact I could have filled a bottle for free at home. The marketing story of how cold bottled water became an actual product that we purchase –even though most of us can get water of equal quality conveniently and without cost – is well documented. I don't intend to retell it here. But as a guy who makes his living thanks to advertising, I think about the bottled water marketing story every time I buy some. When I drop a couple of bucks I try not to think about it. All that I think about is how that cold water tastes great and is so healthy for me. Besides, it comes in that handy little bottle. It says to everyone that I'm in the upper middle-class now. Not to mention, the pretty mountain scene printed on the bottle makes me feel much better about things.

Actually, it's not so much the cost of the water that bothers me. It's not as though paying for water here and there lowers my standard of living. What bothers me is considering how many similar irrational choices I'm making, unaware. Who has subtly convinced me in other areas of my life to do things that don't make financial or logical sense? Is the expensive bottled water just the tip of an iceberg hiding a pattern of undetected irrational behavior? Perhaps, these are questions we are afraid to consider.

So why is it we spend six or seven dollars per gallon of packaged water at the convenience store when we can get it from our tap for free? Why do so many people instantly get on board with the tiring daily outrage or campaign or trend perpetuated on social media? Why do thousands stage protests over an "injustice" that is often rooted in untruth? Why do so many more people buy a lottery ticket when the prize tops a billion dollars, despite the odds remaining infinitesimally poor? Even more serious, how did Adolf Hitler convince so many to adopt and comply with his murderous ideology? Why do politicians all seem to sound the same? Why do cake mixes require two fresh eggs when the manufacturer could include egg powder?

Well, the "why"s are endless, and in this book we try to answer them. More accurately, we try to give you the basis for answering them yourself. Mass messaging in all of its forms – advertising, public relations, packaging and marketing, political campaign messaging, journalism, and every form of mass communication – almost always contains some level of propaganda. Much of it is innocent and benign. But all of it is designed to accomplish something. Knowing what that something is should be a priority for every media consumer.

When you walk into any box store, for example, you are bombarded with literally thousands of messages. Every package on every shelf is an effort to grab your attention. The music playing over the store's public address system has a specific cadence. The lighting, interior design, temperature, and even the store layout – all of them – have a purpose. When you turn on the television, pay attention not only to the advertising – the most overt propaganda – but more importantly to the messages being conveyed when propaganda would normally not be expected. For example, if you're watching a drama, observe the premise, story-line, or plot twists. Listen to how news stories are delivered and written. Pay attention to who's made fun of in a comedy. Who or what is being ridiculed, or praised? What products are they using you don't consciously see? Are certain behaviors depicted as shameful, or preferable? Is there a pattern? If so, how has that pattern, over time, shaped the way you view the world?

We know that not every pixel delivered on television is part of some mass mind control program, and it's not our goal to create obsessive or paranoid media consumers. Yet our media consumption is filled with subtle-but-effective techniques and messages to alter both our perception and behavior relating to our world. We all could stand to be more aware.

This process of propaganda has been around for a very long time. Ancient political leaders and merchants used it routinely. But we have seen a dramatic fine-tuning of the process in the last 100 or so years. The history of perfecting propaganda in the last ten or eleven decades is remarkable with facets that are both interesting and concerning. With the rise of psychology, increased understanding of our subconscious terrain, and the application of modern day science to these inner motivations, propaganda truly has become a science. Combine that with the speed of media today and you'll see that the pace and frequency at which propaganda occurs is mind-numbing.

This book is an effort to equip you with some knowledge and awareness that will hopefully help you make better choices about your purchases, behaviors, and even your opinions. It offers a peek behind the curtain into the

5

sneaky laboratory of social scientists and their capacity to change rational outcomes. Our goal in writing this book is to add to your healthy and constructive scrutiny of the media and marketing that is so often consumed without a second thought.

You truly are, living in spin.

CHAPTER 1: PERSUASION

"Perception is reality."
Lee Atwater (political strategist for George H.W. Bush)

Do you ever get the feeling you're being manipulated? That's because you are. Marketing and propaganda are constant and ubiquitous forces that powerfully exploit mental shortcuts to manipulate us. Mindfulness takes effort. Often, we are too pre-occupied or lazy to maintain constant skepticism of the messages we are given. Like food that doesn't need to be chewed, it is easier to ingest information without evaluating it. This is probably why television was once called "Pablum [a brand of baby food] for the masses." Politicians and marketers are eager to play on our assumptions, taking advantage of our lack of discernment. They rely on our willingness to blindly accept their message without making an effort to critically analyze it. Without constant vigilance, we are easily misled by charismatic leaders like children following a Pied Piper.

Let me demonstrate: Imagine your life as narrated by Morgan Freeman. Suddenly, the mundane seems interesting and important. A trip to the convenience store for a gallon of milk becomes the beginning of a compelling life journey. The fact you forgot your wallet bears profound future significance. Just the sound of Freeman's voice commands your attention because it evokes wisdom and greatness. It draws you in, inviting you to listen and learn.

Morgan Freeman has done an exceptional job of creating and maintaining his image as a wise guide and friend. From his roles as a faithful sidekick in Robin Hood: Prince of Thieves and an insightful advisor in The Shawshank Redemption, to more recent characters like the wise wizard, Vitruvius, in The Lego Movie, you might say he is typecast. In fact, his voice alone has become an iconic brand. Who would be a more appropriate guide to the universe than God himself? Perhaps the fact that Freeman has played God in movies influenced his selection as host of the Science Channel's series Through the Wormhole. Imagine how differently this program would be perceived if it were narrated by Adam Sandler. Just as a narrators voice can lull even the most skeptical audience, the sales pitch or delivery is often as critical as the message itself.

Marketers, admen, and spin doctors know the easiest way to compel others to do something is to make them want to do it. The art of propaganda merely makes a person want to do something they may not otherwise. This requires an adept understanding of motivational psychology. It is no coincidence that propaganda evolved as a science as Freud was delving into our consciousness.

One very influential pioneer in the emerging field of marketing was Edward Bernays.

Born in Vienna to Jewish parents in 1891, he was the nephew of Sigmund Freud from both sides of the family. His mother was Sigmund's sister and his father, Ely Bernays, was the brother of Freud's wife, Martha. "He was as driven as his uncle to know what subconscious forces motivated people, and he used Freud's writings to help him understand. But while the esteemed analyst tried to use psychology to free his patients from emotional crutches, Bernays used it to rob consumers of their free will, helping his clients predict, then manipulate, the very way their customers thought and acted—all of which he openly acknowledged in his writings."[1]

Keenly aware of image, Bernays demurred the title of adman, but was proud to be labeled "The Father of Public Relations." Over his career of several decades, he worked as an advertising consultant for many well-known companies including General Electric, Proctor & Gamble, General Motors, CBS, United

---

1. Tye, L. (2002). The Father of Spin: Edward L. Bernays and the Birth of Public Relations. Picador.

Fruit Company, Metropolitan Life Insurance Company, and American Tobacco Company. He campaigned for fluoridated water for Public Health Services and promoted India's image as a democratic nation. On Woodrow Wilson's "Committee on Public Information" he generated propaganda for American support of World War I. Later, he served as an image consultant for the quiet President Coolidge. Because of Bernays, we eat bacon and eggs for breakfast and hospitals serve Jello.[2] [3] As a clever propagandist, he employed all the tools of the trade including product placement, paid testimonials, press releases, jingles, trend-setting with movie stars, smear campaigns, and even warmongering. His influence shaped American culture, politics, education, and public health during the 20th Century, and it continues today.

During his nearly 80-year career in marketing, Bernays kept careful notes of his daily activities and strategies. He also authored

2. Bernays, E. L. (2005). Propaganda. New York: Ig Publishing, 90.
3. Tye, L. (2002). The Father of Spin: Edward L. Bernays and the Birth of Public Relations. Picador.

several books laying down his ideas regarding manipulation of the masses. With titles like Propaganda, Engineering of Consent, and Crystalizing Public Opinion, his books offer Bernays' frank, and sometimes frightening, perspectives. In explaining the need for propaganda to control human behavior he wrote, "The conscious and intelligent manipulation of the organized habits and opinions of the masses is an important element in democratic society. Those who manipulate this unseen mechanism of society constitute an invisible government which is the true ruling power of our country… It is not usually realized how necessary these invisible governors are to the orderly functioning of our group life…Propaganda is the executive arm of the invisible government."[4]

Bernays advocated for a government of enlightened despotism. Though upsetting, it probably should have come as no surprise to Bernays that his book, Crystallizing Public Opinion, was found in the personal library

4. Bernays, E. L. (2005). Propaganda. New York: Ig Publishing, 37-38, 48

of Joseph Goebbels, the Nazi Reich Minister of Propaganda.[5] In fact, he may have been speaking from premonition when he stated, "[Propaganda] may be abused. It may be used to over-advertise an institution and to create in the public mind artificial values. There can be no absolute guarantee against its misuse."[6]

Sought out and highly paid, Bernays occasionally consulted with his famous uncle. They likely discussed motivational psychology, human behavior, and other topics of mutual interest. Bernays became adept at implementing this knowledge in his advertising campaigns. For example, when hired to increase piano sales, Bernays applied psychology-based propaganda techniques. In his book, Propaganda, Bernays describes the campaign. "… Instead of assaulting sales resistance by direct attack, [the salesman] is interested in removing sales resistance. He creates circumstances

5. Bernays, E. L. (1965). Biography of an Idea: Memoirs of Public Relations Counsel Edward L. Bernays. New York: Simon and Schuster, 652.
6. Bernays, E. L. (2005). Propaganda. New York: Ig Publishing, cover.

which will swing emotional currents so as to make for purchaser demand."

Instead of directly promoting the product, in this case a piano, he promoted a national trend that demanded his merchandise. He organized an exhibition of period music rooms designed by well-known decorators. The rooms were filled with expensive tapestries to create the image of prestige and class. To open the exhibition, he held a highly publicized ceremony with society leaders on the guest lists. Going further, he persuaded influential architects to add a music room to their home designs. Let Bernays describe his goals in his own words: "The music room will be accepted because it has been made the thing. And the man or woman who has a music room… will naturally think of buying a piano. It will come to him as his own idea." [7]

However, Bernays was not the only one applying Freud's ideas to the field of marketing. When sales of Betty Crocker's instant cake mixes stalled, General Mills (Betty Crocker's

7. Bernays, E. L. (2005). Propaganda. New York: Ig Publishing, 77-78.

parent company) brought in Ernest Dichter to suggest improvements.[8] Dichter, another Austrian-American, has been called the "Father of Motivational Research." He coined the term "focus group" for his sessions where consumers were observed using and discussing products. Their responses were analyzed and assisted in product development and marketing. One such session involving children yielded the invention of the Barbie Doll.[9] Influenced by Freudian psychoanalytic techniques, he did not shy away from sexual innuendos. His solution for Betty Crocker was no exception.

After performing one of his focus group sessions, he noted that women felt guilt about the simplicity of the instant cake mix. At the time, all that was required to make the batter was to mix the package contents with water. Women wanted to be more involved with the process. Dichter recommended the mix leave out powdered eggs, requiring women to

8. Marks, S. (2005). Finding Betty Crocker: The Secret Life of America's First Lady. New York: Simon and Schuster, 168.
9. Ames, L. (1998, August 2). The View From Peekskill; Tending the Flame of a Motivator. New York Times.

contribute their own fresh eggs.[10] It probably helped that this change added to the sense of freshness and the quality of the product, but the inference is not subtle.

Psychoanalysts, like Freud, sometimes used free association to explore the subconscious by freely expressing linked thoughts and ideas. They recognized the power of association, whether conscious or subliminal. Associations lay the foundation for assumptions. Ideas become connected and suppositions become facts. The power of association is so great that a lie is not needed. Just let people make assumptions. In nature, harmless snakes sometimes have color patterns that mimic those of venomous snakes. Potential predators see these patterns and just leave them alone because they have connected the color pattern with danger. Humans are usually even more clever and elaborate in their deceptions.

---

10. Shapiro, Laura (2004). Something from the Oven: Reinventing Dinner in the 1950s America. New York:Viking, 74-80.

In the late 1940s, the United States Atomic Energy Commission (AEC) began looking for a site to locate the word's first reactor testing station. By 1949, it had settled on the Naval Proving Ground in Southeast Idaho. The Proving Ground had served as a plant to warehouse ordnance and to manufacture, repair, and test the Navy's massive battleship guns during World War II. Now, the area would serve as a place to test and develop the emerging science of atomic energy.

Once the testing station site was designated, the AEC needed a nearby, but less remote location for its field office. Each of the three adjacent towns recognized the potential economic boon from such a designation and began campaigning with zeal. The winner could expect a tremendous boost in jobs, infrastructure, and economic growth. Leonard "Bill" Johnston was named by the AEC as chief engineer-in-charge and was to select among the towns of Arco, Pocatello, and Idaho Falls. As he toured the communities and attended parties put on by local leaders, he was courted like a debutante visiting an all-male college.

Although Idaho Falls seemed a very attractive suitor, one major detriment was the lack of roads from the town to the selected site. However, this was no problem for a creative Chamber of Commerce. In an interview years later, one local resident recalls the Chamber arranging for county road construction vehicles to "go to the western edge of town where they moved sufficient dirt around to give a convincing impression that the road to [the site] already was under construction... Activity was particularly heavy on the day that the visitors were brought to see for themselves." [11]

Besides mental association leading to leaps of logic, associated ideas can convey strong feelings. Real estate marketers sometimes suggest baking bread or cookies before showing your home. The smell is inviting and evokes feelings and memories of a pleasant

11. Stacy, S. M. (2000). Proving the Principle: A History of the Idaho National Engineering and Environmental Laboratory, 1948-1999. Idaho Falls: Idaho Operations Office of the Department of Energy, 33.

childhood and home life. Emotion and memory are closely linked with stimulation of the senses, particularly hearing and smell. Because non-visual senses can be stimulated without our conscious recognition or consent, we are especially vulnerable to this type of manipulation. Think how much a soundtrack adds to an action scene in the movies or a frightening moment in a thriller. You may even try watching a scary movie with the volume muted. It's dramatically less terrifying.

The Schachter-Singer Theory of Emotion recognized the complex interaction between physical experiences, feelings, memories, and perceptions. This theory states that emotion is based on two factors: physiological arousal and a cognitive label. [12]Instead of recognizing the true source of our physical excitement, we often mistakenly identify a sense of arousal as a feeling or emotion. We then misattribute the emotion to something in our environment. A classic study performed in 1974 by Donald

12. Schachter, S., & Singer, J. (1960). Cognitive, Social, and Physiological Determinants of Emotional State. Psychological Review , 69 (5), 379-399.

Dutton and Arthur Aron provides an ideal illustration.

In their experiment, male participants were interviewed after crossing either a sturdy, low bridge or a high suspension bridge. A female interviewer waited for the participant to cross, then approached the male subjects with a survey. She also gave the participants her phone number "in case they wanted to discuss the survey in more detail when she had more time." The study authors believed the experience of crossing a more precarious bridge would create a physical and emotional response that would be misinterpreted as sexual attraction. By comparing the number of subsequent phone calls the interviewer received and the sexual imagery in survey responses, Dutton and Aron were able to demonstrate support for their hypothesis. [13]

Understanding this concept, also called the Two-part Theory of Emotion, helps explain why clever marketing that appeals to all our

13. Dutton, D. G., & Aron, A. P. (1974). Some Evidence for Heightened Sexual Attraction Under Conditions of High Anxiety. Journal of Personality and Social Psychology , 30 (4), 510-517.

senses is especially effective. It can stimulate emotional purchases, even on big-ticket items such as a home or car. Sights, sounds, and smells are powerful promotional tools. You may notice that movie theatres often pop more buttery-smelling popcorn, even when they have plenty on hand. Understanding this theory may prompt you to plan a heart-pounding activity for your next date.

As you read this book, I challenge you to consider how the principles apply in your life and your circumstances. Learning to recognize how you may be manipulated gives you power to overcome these forces. Be mindful of the subtle messages that influence your decisions. Develop a healthy skepticism about media and politics. Do you "go with the flow," or leave your brain on autopilot? Recognize times you may be especially vulnerable to a covert message. We seek out entertainment when we need a mental break, decreasing our efforts of critical analysis. When given information, consider the motivations of the messenger. Think about your own motivations and desires and become more thoughtful about achieving them. Refuse to relinquish your freedom to those who are more than willing to make decisions for you.

CHAPTER 2: HERD MENTALITY

"Humanity is mind-controlled and only slightly more conscious than your average zombie."
David Icke

In the past, all clothing and fashion was "couture:" individually crafted and made-to-fit. It was normal for clothing to suit one's individual body type or design tastes because the owner of the clothing was also likely the one creating it. However, individual tastes and styles became a problem with the development of mass production. As companies churned out thousands of products of the same design, they were banking on a receptive public. If they misjudged popular tastes and their product was not accepted, the investment loss could be devastating. Good marketing suddenly became as important as developing a good product.

Wise manufactures realized it would be more profitable to actually create the trends, rather than attempt to follow or adjust to them. Then, they would inform the public what to purchase to be in fashion: their product. The clothing being manufactured would dictate the popular fashion, rather than vice versa. This ensured successful reception of a product or style, or at least made it more likely.

This extended beyond clothing fashion and into all realms of mass production. For example, as Henry Ford pioneered improvements in mass production, he recognized the importance of dictating the tastes of the day. In his own autobiography, he quotes himself as saying, "Any customer can have a car painted any colour (sic) he wants so long as it is black."[1]

This exclusivity to black came with the adoption of the assembly line in his factories.

1 Ford, H. (1922). My Life and Work. A Public Domain Book.

As production speed increased, he found the time it took the paint to dry was the limiting step in how quickly a car could be manufactured. Because black dried the fastest, other colors previously available were discontinued. After the adoption of the assembly line (and the color black), a Model T Ford could be produced in 93 minutes. Prior to that it took over 12 hours per car.[2] Cost likely was also a factor as black cars were cheaper to produce and had a higher profit margin. The black Model T became so ubiquitous, when Ford later produced the Model A, a superior car by many measures, he intentionally avoided the color black the first few years of production.

By the 1920's, the Model T had fallen behind the competition technologically and was seen as an automobile of the lower socioeconomic classes. Sales dropped off dramatically as other manufacturers produced more advanced automobiles. With a keen sense of marketing, Ford insisted the new, updated Model A would

2 Georgano, N. (1985). Cars: Early and Vintage 1886-1930. London: Grange-Universal.

be available in colors other than black. Instead of progressing down the alphabet with the next model, he also chose to start again at the letter "A" to signify a car so different, it would be a reset for Ford Motor Company.

As a side note, Henry Ford did not "invent the assembly line" as he is often credited, just as Edison did not "invent the light bulb." This itself is an example of propaganda allowed by his icon status and propagated by the oversimplification of history education. Public education thrives on jingle-like factoids that force students and teachers into True and False questions, rather than an accurate and complete answer in essay form. (More on propaganda in education in Chapter 7)

Sometimes efforts to create demand from the masses backfire or have unintended consequences. I recently overheard an advertisement for a new all-natural cereal made from Quinoa (pronounced Keen-wa). Later that day, while grocery shopping, I noticed what looked like a bag of very expensive bird food with the funny word "Quinoa" on its label. Until that day, I had never heard of quinoa. Two thoughts entered my brain. The first, "I need to remember that Q-word for my next game of Scrabble." The second, "what is behind this sudden explosion of quinoa on the market?" A few years ago, the product was essentially unheard of by the general public, and now it seems ubiquitous. This aroused my suspicions, so I had to look into it.

Quinoa is an edible seed originating from the costal mountains of South America. Initially cultivated for human consumption about 4,000 years ago, it has served as a food staple in Andean cultures for centuries and was considered sacred by the Incans. It is relatively easy to grow in cool, arid conditions and provides a good source of nutrition. So, how did this humble seed become a superstar?

In short, the UN reached down from its high and holy place and anointed the lowly quinoa as a solution to world hunger. The United Nations General Assembly named 2013 the "International Year of Quinoa." The resolution adopted by the 193-member body explains the desire to recognize the Andean indigenous people "who have managed to preserve quinoa in its natural state as food for present and future generations, through ancestral practices of living in harmony with nature."[3] The seed was quickly labeled a "superfood," a marketing term with no scientific basis. Unfortunately, in their ambitions to recognize quinoa and the stewardship of the indigenous people, they may have elevated quinoa beyond the reach of its stewards.

According to records from the Bolivian government, quinoa consumption has decreased by 1/3 in just 5 years. One villager states, "We produce quinoa just for export. It's more profitable."[4] By some estimates, quinoa prices have increased eight-fold. It is more affordable for growers to sell and use the money to purchase other, often foreign foods--usually with less nutritional value. In Peru, it has become a luxury product. The increased value of this crop has

3 United Nations. (2013, February 20). UN News Centre. Retrieved January 20, 2016, from http://www.un.org/apps/news/story.asp?NewsID=44184#.VFZ36SE9KSN
4 Collyns, D. (2013, January 14). Quinoa Brings Riches to the Andes. The Guardian.

also increased land conflicts by local farmers, changed ancient farming techniques resulting in increased resource consumption, and diluted the indigenous culture. These effects seem counter to the intent of the UN Counsel and, ironically, undo the very virtues the General Assembly meant to praise and extoll.

Another paradoxical manipulation of the masses occurred when Edward Bernays used trendsetting techniques to turn addictive, enslaving cigarettes into "Torches of Freedom." In 1929 he staged a PR stunt at the New York City Easter Parade that would unravel a major social taboo and change the laws of the land. At the time, it was illegal in New York for women to smoke in public. George Washington Hill, president of American Tobacco Company, hired Bernays to promote the "Lucky Strike" brand and specifically directed him to entice more women to smoke. Bernays turned to shills to orchestrate the movement. He paid attractive women to defy the social mores by lighting up cigarettes, or as he dubbed them--"Torches of Freedom," while marching in the parade. Leading up to the event, he tipped off the press about the upcoming "newsworthy event." He even directed the photo and camera shots to ensure thorough and compelling coverage. From there, the crowd followed and the image of women smoking became sexy and sophisticated. [5] [6] As an ironic side note, Bernays' wife later died from lung cancer related to cigarette smoking.

A "shill" is defined as "an accomplice of a hawker, gambler, or swindler who acts as an enthusiastic customer to entice or encourage others." We often refer to them as a "plant" or a "stooge." They're the loud and excited customers ooo-ing and awww-ing on infomercials. Politicians often use them to ask scripted questions at rallies and stump speeches.

On a lovely October morning in 2013, President Obama gave a speech touting the success

5. Curtis, A. (Writer), & Curtis, A. (Director). (1997). The Century of Self [Motion Picture]. BBC.
6. 1929 Torches of Freedom. (n.d.). Retrieved December 11, 2015, from The Museum of Public Relations: http://www. PRMuseum.com

of the Affordable Care Act. Behind him stood a wall of beautiful, hand selected representatives of the formerly uninsured. Each had a personal story of the benevolent role Obamacare played in their lives, rescuing them from insurance company rejection due to pre-existing conditions. Just over the President's right shoulder in perfect frame of the camera and wearing an attractive red dress stood a young pregnant woman. Several minutes into the speech she began to swoon, just in time for Obama to show his caring side and come to her rescue. Right away, many people questioned if she was a shill.[7] Even before the snake-oil salesman, there were shills. The fact that they endure is testament to their effectiveness and evidence of herd mentality. It just takes a little skepticism to begin seeing them everywhere.

After being introduced to the idea of "shills" in a Sociology class, two intrigued high school students set out to test this newly discovered power of social influence. Of course,

7. Larsen, L. (2013, October 22). Pregnant Diabetic Who Nearly Fainted at Obamacare Speech Denies Stunt Claims. New York Daily News.

the natural laboratory chosen by the teenagers was the local mall. They set their sites on a kiosk selling custom T-shirts. At the kiosk, the customers could design a shirt with the picture or slogan of their choice and the salesman would have it silkscreened for them. After finding their target, the students stood back and just watched. Over the next ten minutes, the salesman tried several times to entice passersby with no success, so the students stepped in to help. They casually wandered past and allowed the salesman to make his pitch. Showing just a little interest at first, they stopped to listen. The salesman smiled. After his spiel, the teenagers asked a few questions and began talking amongst themselves. Two other pedestrians began to eavesdrop. Then, the teens dialed up the enthusiasm.

Becoming more animated, they began to share ideas for clever designs, witty slogans, or silly puns to have printed on the shirt. Laughing and making a game of it, they soon had a crowd gathering. Suspecting crowd may just be there for entertainment and not to make a purchase, one student then directed his efforts to make a sale. He began picking out colors and shirt sizes, acting concerned they may not have enough to print all the shirts he would want. "Oh, these will make great gifts!" he told his friend.

Soon others were grabbing up shirts and taking out their wallets. Before the two students left the kiosk, three customers had made purchases. The ringleader later admitted he felt a little guilty for manipulating the crowd, but the customers were laughing and seemed very pleased with the product. It doesn't take much to be a trendsetter. In fact, as Bernays explained, "the group mind does not think in the strict sense of the word. In place of thoughts it has impulses, habits, and emotions. In making up its mind, its first impulse is usually to follow the example of a trusted leader. This is one of the most firmly established principles of mass psychology." [8]

Although we can all imagine this technique being used by slimy salespeople hawking

8. Bernays, E. L. (2005). Propaganda. New York: Ig Publishing, 73.

useless products, we don't really think about successful CEOs relying on shills. Apparently it happens. In a study published by the National Bureau of Economic Research of Cambridge, Massachusetts, four financial professors found that CEOs use the media to boost sales of their newly vested stocks. Here's how it works: As part of their compensation, CEOs are often given company stock, but must wait a specified period of time before they can sell the stock. When the stocks become eligible for sale, they are called "vested."

Companies offer stocks as compensation for a variety of reasons. One purpose is to motivate the CEO to make the company profitable, thus increasing the value of his or her own stock. It gives the CEO "skin in the game." However, as the study demonstrated, it may also motivate the CEO to manipulate the system. Instead of a sustained effort over years to maximize the company's success, the CEO may focus on a brief spike in value just as the stock becomes vested. They turn to their accomplices in the media to carry out the con.

"The study authors found not only that significantly more discretionary corporate news is released in a typical CEO's vesting months than non-vesting months, but also that the news released in those months has a significantly more positive tone than news released at other times."[9] The positive news draws the attention of a crowd of investors and stock prices jump. The CEO then sells his vested holdings for a big payout (often in the millions). This is unnervingly similar to an illegal activity traders call the "pump and dump."

The problem with the idea of herd behavior is that it is based on humans behaving at the level of instinct, emotion, and lust. It overlooks our divine human qualities that lift us above these ignoble drives. Human beings do have the ability to think and act for themselves. We are not animals, as Bernays believed. Cows follow a herd, birds stay with their flock, but humans are called "homo sapiens" for a reason. It means "wise man."

9. Hulbert, M. (2014, November 6). CEOs Manipulate News for Personal Gain, Study Finds. Barrons.

Following the ideology of mentors like Walter Lippmann and Gustove LeBon (the originator of crowd psychology), Bernays felt the average person was unable to handle the responsibility of personal decision making. He saw humans as illogical, obtuse, and (a word he used often) "stupid."[10] Although not entirely accurate, the adage is that the average human only use about 10% of his or her brain. Maybe the problem is we are only thinking critically about 10% of the time. We become mentally lazy, relinquishing power to those willing to make decisions for us.

"In theory, every citizen makes up his mind on public questions and matters of private conduct. In practice, if all men had to study for themselves the abstruse economic, political, and ethical data involved in every question, they would find it impossible to come to a conclusion without anything. We have voluntarily agreed to let an invisible government sift the data and high-spot the outstanding issue so that our field of choice shall be narrowed to

10. Curtis, A. (Writer), & Curtis, A. (Director). (1997). The Century of Self [Motion Picture]. BBC.

practical proportions. From our leaders and the media they use to reach the public, we accept the evidence and the demarcation of issues bearing upon public question."[11] This sounds a bit like North Korea's "Dear Leader" speaking, but these are Bernays' words.

Though a master of crowd psychology, Edward Bernays' Achilles heel was the individual. Peter Strauss, a former employee of Bernays, explains, "He was uniquely knowledgeable about how people in large numbers were going to react, but... he didn't have any sense for reaching out to people one-on-one...He didn't think about people in groups of one. He thought about people in groups of thousands."[12]

Even Bernays himself admitted with frustration, "It is sometimes possible to change the attitudes of millions, but impossible to change the attitude of one man."[13] The key to weakening propaganda is to think for ourselves. This

11. Bernays, E. L. (2005). Propaganda. New York: Ig Publishing, 38.
12. Curtis, A. (Writer), & Curtis, A. (Director). (1997). The Century of Self [Motion Picture]. BBC.
13. Tye, L. (2002). The Father of Spin: Edward L. Bernays and the Birth of Public Relations. Picador.

requires effort, but our freedom is worth it. We need to question the message, do our own research, and carefully consider the facts. We must take responsibility for our actions and maintain our individual liberty.

CHAPTER 3: WHAT'S IN A NAME?

"…he explained the name was the important thing for inspiring the necessary fear. You see, no one would surrender to the Dread Pirate Westley."

The Man in Black, The Princess Bride, 1987

- Night—light
- Kill—kiss

These words are vastly different in meaning, though only separated by a single sound. A phoneme (pronounced foh-neem) is the smallest unit of language which changes the meaning of a word, as in the above examples.[1] Derived from Ancient Greek, the word phoneme literally means "utterance" and was first used in the 1870s by linguists to refer to a speech sound.[2] So, how does this obscure concept relate to propaganda? In the 1920s, an inquisitive young linguist recognized the surprising power of the phoneme. Most linguists at the time were recording, categorizing, and organizing language with the objective focus of an accountant. However, Edward Sapir was a linguistic genius, inspired by the magic of words and sounds in evoking thoughts and feelings.[3] Based on Sapir's insight, an expanded definition of "phoneme" may be "the smallest unit of propaganda."

Edward Sapir's origins are much like those of Edward Bernays. Born in 1884 to a Jewish family in Prussia, Edward Sapir's first language

1. Liddell, H. G., & Scott, R. (1996). A Greek-English Lexicon. (H. S. Jones, & R. McKenzie, Trans.) Oxford: Clarendon Press.
2. Twaddell, W. F. (1935). On Defining the Phoneme. Language , 11 (1), 5-62
3. Harris, Z. S. (1951). Methods of Structural Linguistics. Chicago: Chicago University Press.

was Yiddish. When he was four, his family emigrated to England, then two years later, moved to the United States. Though the family was not orthodox, his father, Jacob Sapir, used music to maintain the family connection to its Jewish heritage. Raised in poverty, primarily by his working mother following his parents' divorce, he also lost his brother to typhoid fever as a child. At fourteen, his dedication and intelligence earned him a Pulitzer scholarship. Instead of using the scholarship money to attend a prestigious school, he chose a more economical high school and contributed the money to help support his family.[4]

He went on to Columbia University where he studied Latin, Greek, French, Sanskrit, Danish, Swedish, Old Saxon, Gothic, Germanic languages, and Icelandic. This is also where he was introduced to Native American languages and mythology, a major focus of his studies for the remainder of his life. In fact, he would go on to spend years living among indigenous

4. Darnell, R. (2010). Edward Sapir: Linguist, Anthropologist, Humanist. University of Nebraska Press.

people of North America, creating a record of their language and culture. His fervor in this pursuit could be compared to a conservationist studying an endangered species in its natural habitat. Indeed, his work captured some of these languages and histories as they became "extinct." Just as Sapir's father used Jewish songs to preserve the family's heritage as Lithuanian Jews, Sapir studied traditional Native American songs and folklore to document the language.

In our lives, we can all recognize turning points where seemingly small experiences or events completely transform us by changing our perspective. For Edward Sapir, it wasn't until his final year in college that he found a mentor and teacher in Franz Boaz. This influence would profoundly alter his perspectives regarding language and was key in his connection of language and culture. Franz Boaz, a man often regarded as the "Father of American Anthropology" may have created this pivot point for Sapir by allowing him to enroll in his graduate-level course on Anthropology, though Sapir was still an undergraduate. Other students of Franz Boaz include Ruth Benedict, Margaret Mead, and Zora Neale Hurston.[5]

While pioneering the connection between anthropology and linguistics, Sapir published an illustrative paper based on the idea of the phoneme. His unique background in both fields sparked his initial insight into the psychology of word sounds. His fieldwork allowed him the format to experiment and test his theories. In his 1929 "A Study in Phonetic Symbolism," Sapir examined the relationship between word sounds (phonemes) and presumed characteristics. He asked subjects to associate two invented words "mil" and "mal" with a small and a large table. An overwhelming majority (80%) of subjects linked the small table with the word "mil," while assigning "mal" to the large table. This landmark study has been the springboard for further research in sound symbolism.[6]

5. Moore, J. D. (2012). Visions of Culture: An Introduction to Anthropological Theories and Theorists. AltaMira Press.
6. Sapir, E. (1929). A Study in Phonetic Symbolism. Journal of Experimental Psychology , 12 (3), 225-239.

Sapir went on to propose an explanation for the consistent linking of certain sounds to specific characteristics. He believed these associations were related to mouth shape when forming sounds, the volume, and the pitch of various phonemes. Building on this foundation, researchers have created amazingly accurate algorithms to predict association of meanings with phonemes. In a study published decades after Sapir's death, Richard Klink found "both vowels and consonants of [fictitious] brand names were able to communicate product-related information in the absence of any marketing communications."

For example, given no other information about an imaginary product except brand name, Klink found that motorcycles named "Valp" were rated as faster, lighter in color, and less heavy than motorcycles branded as "Galp." "Tidip" brand shampoo was perceived to be more feminine and softer than "Todip" shampoo. Sapir's gifted insight that these associations transcend language and culture are echoed in the study as well. "As mentioned, evidence suggests forms of sound symbolism are not language-specific and, therefore, may be particularly informative in naming products that compete globally."[7] Now more than ever, these principles are actively studied and used to develop successful trade names and products.

Drug companies are especially busy searching for brand names that will create confidence in the medications they develop. Adding to the challenge, several regulatory organizations such as the Food & Drug Administration (FDA), the Patent ant Trademark Office (PTO), and the European Medicines Agency (EMEA) apply restrictions on what names will be approved. In facts, it is estimated that over 1/3 of names submitted to the FDA are rejected while the EMEA declines about ½ of submissions. Names cannot suggest superiority, safety, or off-label uses. They must also be distinct enough from existing names to avoid confusion. Drug companies must also ensure

7. Klink, R. R. (2000). Creating Brand Names with Meaning: The Use of Sound Symbolism. Marketing Letters , 11 (1), 5-20.

the name translates well to other languages and cultures. In fact, the EMEA "forbids the approval of drug names that sound offensive in any European Union language." With all this in mind, it is no surprise that pharmaceutical companies reportedly spend anywhere from $250,000 to $2.5 million just to develop a new medicine's name.[8]

Building on Sapir's early research, brand marketers turn to well-researched algorithms to assist in this process. It's commonly asserted that the consonant sounds "k," "z," "q," "p," "t," and "d" convey strength and reliability. "L," "r," "m," and "s" are soothing and relaxing. Marketers also believe that letters like "z" make drugs sound faster while "f" makes them sound softer. Certain letters and sounds are also associated with feminine or masculine traits. "Sound symbolism shows that the sounds of words still convey meaning. More important, consumers recognize this phonetic

8. Dutchen, S. (2009, January 24). Retrieved October 20, 2015, from Scope: http://www.scopeweb.mit.edu/articles/a-drug-by-any-other-name/

meaning and will use it as a source of product information."[9]

Think of the prescription sleeping pill called "Ambien." At first, it seems like just another trade name with no specific meaning, chosen nearly at random. However, if you look closely at the Ambien logo, you will find clues that tell a different story.

First, notice how the first two letters "A" and "M" are in bold. It is subtle, so look closely. Then the "B" is a little bigger although it is right in the middle of the word. These small changes cue our brain to see

this word as "A.M. Bien." We can think of the A.M. as "morning." The wave above the word "~" is not just a meaningless brushstroke. It's a tilde. We don't really use it much in English, but in Spanish it is used to make the "enye" or ñ. In the logo, the tilde signals to the brain, "think Spanish." From there, we translate the

9. Yorkston, E., & Menon, G. (2004). A Sound Idea: Phonetic Effects of Brand Names on Consumer Judgements. Journal of Consumer Research, 31.

"Bien" to "good." Put all this together and we come up with A.M. Bien—"morning good" or "good morning" from the trade name Ambien. Presumably, the message is if you take Ambien, you will sleep well and have a "good morning."

It's not just pharmaceuticals that play the name game. During the 19th Century, rapeseed oil was primary used as a lubricant for steam engines. Due to its bitter taste, it was not particularly useful for consumption. In the late 1970s, Canadian scientists used cross-breeding techniques to decrease the oil's high levels of glucosinolates, the source of bitterness. In the process, it created a more healthy blend of fats, including monounsaturated fats and Omega-3 fatty acids. However, it wasn't just the taste of rapeseed oil that consumers found offensive. Marketers needed to come up with a more palatable name to sell the public on their product. "Rapeseed" became "Canola," derived from "Canada" and "oil." [10]

---

10. Canola Council of Canada. (n.d.). The History of Canola. Retrieved January 20, 2016, from http://www.canolacouncil. org/oil-and-meal/what-is-canola/the-history-of-canola/

People names are no less important than brand or product names. Think of the one thing all children receive from their parents, whether rich or poor, and carry with them throughout their entire lifetime. What is the first thing that most people know about you, thus creating their first impression? It is your name. Studies have been done to compare the sounds and symbols in the names of presidential candidates to determine electability with some degree of accuracy. More importantly, names carry strong connotations of character and personality. Perhaps this is why many parents spend months deliberating on a child's name. Unfortunately, it seems that sometimes parents painfully miss the mark in trying to be clever or unique. A name is a brand and thoughtfulness in bestowing a name would be wise.

It's possible the television star and physician "Dr. Oz" owes some of his success to his name. His full name, Mehmet Cengiz Oz, isn't the easiest brand name to promote, especially in a post-9/11 America where middle-Eastern origins may be a professional liability. However, for most Americans, the name "Oz" more likely stirs a reminiscence of "The Great Oz," a wise ruler in a land somewhere over the rainbow. This Oz, though later found to be a charade, was sought after as an all-knowing wizard. Whether the connection is consciously recognized or remains as a subconscious character reference, the name likely helps create an aura of wisdom. (I do find it interesting he often wears scrubs for the filming of his television programs, as though he just walked out of the operating room and into the studio. Once again, it's part of the image.)

To continue the discussion about the importance of names, it is important to examine the role of euphemisms. Common in all realms, euphemisms are especially ubiquitous in law, medicine, and politics. Euphemism is commonly used when the actual word or idea is repulsive, unpleasant, or offensive. It seems the uglier or nastier the subject, the more it is replaced by euphemism. One graphic example is the word "poo." There are hundreds of words to stand in for "poo." We use "feces", "night soil," "mess," "waste," "dung," "#2," "turd," "doo-doo," "stool," and "excrement." To the entomologist, it is "frass" or "castings." An ornithologist refers to "droppings." A nurse calls it a "bowel movement," or simply "BM," while a doctor may use "stercus." Even more descriptive terms include "hematochezia" for bloody stool and "melena" for black stool. Paleontologists refer to "coprolites," spelunkers say "guano," biologists use "scat," and farmers call it "manure."

With careful wordsmithing, evil acts, gruesome diseases, and maleficent intentions are also dressed up and made palatable, much like a wolf in sheep's clothing. Roy Peter Clark, a well-respected writing coach and teacher observed, "It was…George Orwell who posited a direct relationship between political corruption and the misuse of language…Orwell's attention was fixed on language at the level of words and phrases: the use of euphemism to veil unspeakable horrors…"[11] In fact, a synonym for euphemism, "doublespeak," derives from a combination of the terms "doublethink" and "newspeak" found in Orwell's novel 1984.

The Vietnam War was referred to as a "police action." [12] Affirmative Action disguises discrimination.[13] North Korea has its "work camps" and Nazi's had their "concentrations camps."[14] Government spending becomes "investment." Gonorrhea, a common sexually transmitted bacterial infection that can cause pain, foul discharge, infertility, meningitis,

11. Clark, R. P. (2012, February 20). How "Narrative" Moved from Literature to Politics & What This Means for Covering Candidates. Retrieved October 20, 2015, from Poynter: http://www.poynter.org/2012/how-narrative-moved-from-literature-to-politics-what-this-means-for-covering-candidates/162834/

12. Truman, H. S. (1950, June 29). The President's News Conference of June 29, 1950. Retrieved January 3, 2016, from Teaching American History: http://teachingamerican-history.org/library/document/the-presidents-news-conference-of-june-29-1950/

13. Custred, G. (2001, May 22). Affirmative Action: A Euphemism for Racial Profiling by Government. Investor's Business Daily.

14. Flanagan, E., & Yoo, J. (2014, February 18). Life in a North Korean Labor Camp: 'No Thinking … Just Fear'. Retrieved March 4, 2015, from NBCNews.com: http://nbcnews.com/news/world/life-north-korean-labor-camp-no-thinking-just-fear-n32076

and blindness in newborns is simply called "The Clap." Aborting a baby has become "terminating a pregnancy." Drake Baer of Business Insider recently listed 48 examples of euphemisms for getting fired. Some of them bordered on ridiculous, like "decruited," "excessed," "fumigation," "outplacement," and the verbose "career assessment and re-employment."[15] It likely doesn't feel any better to lose your job to "downsizing" rather than mass layoffs, and "enhanced interrogation" probably feels a lot like torture.

15. Baer, D. (2014, July 31). 'Indefinate Idling,' 'Redirected,' and 46 Other Euphemisms We Use in Place of 'Fired'. Business Insider.

CHAPTER 4: "WE ARE LEGION"

"...the loveliest trick of the Devil is to persuade you that he does not exist!"
Charles Pierre Baudelaire

This chapter on product placement and subliminal advertising is likely the most challenging to write. Not because there is a paucity of examples. No, they are legion. The challenge arises because admen are usually very secretive in their work. Like a doctor or priest, they often have a code of confidentiality. For that reason, most of the examples and ideas in this chapter are drawn from observation. Source documentation will be limited. Except in rare cases like the braggadocios Edward Benays, it is nearly impossible to find records of marketing strategy from the boardroom.

Perhaps the admen have taken a page from Satan's playbook. The devil's sophistry is promoted by his subtlety. People prefer to believe they are making their own choices freely and resent being manipulated. Advertising and propaganda is more effective when it goes undetected. When product placement is too obvious or intrusive it is often viewed negatively or even willfully resisted. The movie Talladega Nights is humorously based on over-the-top product endorsement. At one point, the main character even inserts a sponsor's plug into his prayer at the dinner table. Though a ridiculous exaggeration, it strikes a chord with the audience because we have all recognized times when marketing is shamelessly overt. Successful advertising gets noticed, but not noted--seen, but not recognized.

One clever and unique example of product placement occurred in the romantic comedy,

"Hitch." Alex Hitchens, the protagonist played by Will Smith, is undone by a sedated, secret-spilling fugue brought on by Benadryl. As he drinks from the cartoon-like, oversized bottle of Benadryl, you may think that is the incident of product placement, but it is more complex than that. Although it probably saved his life, the side effects from this product essential ruin things for him. Now if he had only taken Allegra, a non-sedating antihistamine, things would have been completely different. Interestingly enough, his beautiful love interest is named Allegra Cole. Rather than flashing the product label in your face for a few seconds, the creative script repeated the product's name throughout the movie, along with the positive association with an attractive woman. It's almost like a plot-based subliminal message.

As entertainment and technology evolve, so do the marketing schemes. In times past, movies and television shows placed a specific brand of soda in a scene or had the main character drive a specific model of vehicle. Often, the camera would pan across an advertisement or logo. Now, tech companies have software programmed to insert any product, brand, or logo into still images and video. After identifying the appropriate region or demographic, advertisements can be tailored and adjusted accordingly. For example, a television show originally airing at 5 pm may promote Sprite, but when re-run at 10 pm, the Sprite could digitally be replaced by a Coors Light. As television viewing shifts more toward on-demand or on-line systems like Netflix, this adaptability becomes even more pertinent. For example, this technology was used to insert up-to-date ads into rerun episodes of How I Met Your Mother years after the TV series was originally filmed.[1]

Technology's influence on product placement is not just limited to movies and TV. Each of the millions of iPhones sold is pre-loaded with Disney.com among the "Favorite" websites. This is obviously a paid advertisement and can

1. Souppouris, A. (2014, October 22). Technology Changed Product Placement (And You Didn't Even Notice). Retrieved April 1, 2015, from engadget: http://www.engadget.com/2014/10/22/technology-changed-product-placement/

easily be recognized and deleted by the user, if they desire. However, Siri seems to have a few more advertising tricks up her sleeve.

One interesting update with iOS 8 is predictive text. As you are typing, words and phrases appear and allow you to tap on the correct guess, quickly inserting these words into your text. Like any good personal assistant, it "learns" your vocabulary, names of your friends, and other data to provide useful suggestions. However, when you type "m" into a text message on an Apple device, "m&m" and "m&ms" are the first suggestions. Given that my iPhone has figured out my children's names and offers those as suggestions when I type in their first initial, it seems highly unlikely this is a random guess at what I intend to type. If the suggestion of m&ms is flashed before our eyes, even as a passing word on a screen, will we begin to "randomly" crave little chocolate candies? Thirty years after missing a marketing opportunity with the E.T. movie, M&Ms may have learned a few things.

Product placement is big business, so it's no surprise conflicts among sponsors have reached international levels. At the 2014 FIFA World Cup, Sony was the official sponsor, but that didn't stop many soccer stars from sporting the competing brand "Beats" headphones. The fact that Sony forced FIFA to institute a ban on them probably only added to their appeal. Players seen wearing them during warm-ups were perceived as rebels with sincere and unwavering commitment to their brand of choice. But was it really their choice, or just another sponsorship?

During the 2012 Olympics in London, Beats Electronics sent thousands of free headphones to competing athletes, despite Panasonic being the official sponsor. [2] Although Beats headphones are relatively expensive (usually starting above $200), overall the "free headphone" campaign probably cost the company less than an official sponsorship of the Games. A similar battle was also fought in the NFL between the official

2. Israel, E. (2014, June 17). Soccer-Banned Headphones, a World Cup Fashion Beat. Reuters.

sponsor (Bose) and Beats by Dre.[3] One 49ers player was even fined $10K for violating the Beats ban, making headlines on all the sports pages. When asked if his endorser (Beats Electronics) paid the fine, he stated, "I'm going to let that be unanswered."[4] Ten thousand is a great price for all that publicity.

The James Bond movie, Die Another Day (2002) lies at the other end of the spectrum regarding cost for paid advertising. With a reported $70 million worth of product placement, it was nicknamed by some, "Buy Another Day."[5] It may be difficult to imagine a few moments of advertising being worth that price, but James Bond makes a remarkable spokesman for any product desiring association with sophistication, class, and sex appeal. His allure, based on his confident image, speaks to

3. Breech, J. (2014, October 5). NFL Bans Players from Wearing 'Beats by Dre' Headphones Around Cameras. Retrieved June 8, 2015, from CBS Sports: http://www.mweb. cbssports.com/nfl/eye-on-football/24738617

4. Gutierrez, P. (2014, October 13). Colin Kaepernick Fined $10K. Retrieved August 21, 2015, from ESPN: http://www. espn.go.com/_/id/11671032/

5. Product Placement. (2010, May). Retrieved from Georgian National Film Center: http://www.gnfc.ge/uploads/files/ Product%20Placement2.pdf

men and women of all ages, nationalities, and economic status.

Lest you think these tricks of clandestine propaganda and marketing are a new development arising from increased technology, let me offer another example. You probably don't realize it, but the popular board game "Monopoly" was developed as a tool for promoting a specific political agenda. As originally conceived by Elizabeth Maggie around 1903 and patented as "The Landlord's Game" in 1904, the game was intended to promote the political philosophies of Georgism.[6]

In an era of titans like John D. Rockefeller, Andrew Carnegie, John Jacob Astor, and J. P. Morgan, many Americans were bothered by the apparent disparity between the filthy rich and the working poor. Born in 1839, Henry George, the founder of Georgism, was not immune to the idea of industrialists being labeled "robber barons." He felt the billionaire tycoons had

6. Gayle, D. (2015, February 17). "The Real Story Behind Monopoly: How a Secretary Designed the Board Game More Than 100 Years Ago in Protest Against Property Moguls of the Day. Retrieved January 22, 2016, from Daily Mail Online: http://www.dailymail.co.uk/news/article-2957197/

built their fortunes on the backs of the working class, grinding them deeper into poverty.[7]

The founding tenet of Georgism is that, as industrialized nations progress, the rich became richer and the poor became poorer. This conclusion was based on George's observations as he traveled the newly-expanded United States from East to West. He noted that in older, more established urban areas, such as New York City, the poor were much worse off than the poor in newly settled areas like San Francisco. Based on this conclusion, he believed the only way to remedy this injustice was to develop a system to redistribute wealth. (Does any of this sound familiar?) His proposal was to heavily tax land and resources, as he felt these commodities belonged to all people in common.[8] (Got Communism?)

Georgism, a spark to the Progressive Era,

7. Council of Georgist Organizations. (n.d.). An Introduction to Georgist Philosophy and Activity. Retrieved January 22, 2016, from http://www.cgocouncil.org/cwho.html
8. George, H. (1881). Progress and Poverty: An Inquiry into the Cause of Industrial Depressions and of Increase of Want with Increase of Wealth: The Remedy. New York: D. Appleton and Company.

had many well-known and influential propo-
nents. Among those that commonly make the
list are George Bernard Shaw, Helen Keller,
Franklin D. Roosevelt, Leo Tolstoy, Woodrow
Wilson, Albert Einstein, Upton Sinclair, and
Martin Luther King, Jr.[9] [10] [11] [12] [13]Also includ-
ed is Elizabeth Maggie, creator of "The
Landlord's Game."

Elizabeth, or "Lizzie" as she was known, was
a strong advocate for Georgism, but recognized the ideas and philosophies at its root were
complex and made for heavy dinnertime conver-
sation. Nonetheless, she made it her mission
to thrust these principles into the daily life of
the American public. Wisely, she chose a more

9. Shaw, G. B. (1949). Sixteen Self Sketches: How I Became a
Public Speaker. London: Constable and Company.
10.Wonder Woman at Massey Hall: Helen Keller Spoke to
Large Audience Who Were Spellbound. (1914, January).
Toronto Star Weekly.
11. Wenzer, K. C. (1997). Tolstoy's Georgist Spiritual Political
Economy (1897-1910): Anarchrism and Land Reform. The
American Journal of Economics and Sociology , 56 (4).
12. Einstein, A. (2016, January 22). Two Letters Written in
1934 to Henry George's Daughter, Anna George De Mille.
Retrieved from Cooperative Individualism: http://www.
cooperativeindividualism.org
13. Yglesias, M. (2013, August 28). Martin Luther King's
Case for a Guaranteed Basic Income. Slate.

entertaining format and "repackaged" the ideas as game to influence an unsuspecting audience.

With modern conveniences like indoor plumbing, electric appliances, and rapid transportation, Americans were beginning to have more leisure time. As more homes were wired with indoor lighting, people could stay up later into the night. Maggie capitalized on this increased time to socialize by giving them something enjoyable to do together. "The Landlord's Game," later becoming "Monopoly," exploded in popularity as a covert proselytization for Georgism.[14]

****

As traditional 30 or 60 second television commercials lose affect to the fast-forward button on DVR or are lost altogether with reruns downloaded via the internet, intrusive product placement in other formats will only increase. Internet pop-ups, banner ads, and other annoying advertisements will continue to evolve and become more sophisticated as

14. Pilon, M. (2015, March 3). Ever Cheat at Monopoly? So Did Its Creator: He Stole the Idea from a Woman. NPR: Morning Edition. (D. Green, Interviewer)

marketers learn how to compete for our attention. The format may change as we transition into a more mobile society, but marketing and propaganda will continue to insert itself with even greater potency as the technology to gain entry into our every day lives increases.

CHAPTER 5: JINGLES & SLOGANS & NARRATIVES, OH MY!

"...all this is true because it rhymes."
Vitruvius, The Lego Movie

There is something about a catchy jingle that somehow lowers our defenses against propaganda. It seems to lull our reason and logic like a spell, leaving us vulnerable to even the most ridiculous message. The courtroom scene with O.J. Simpson feigning a struggle to put on bloody gloves, then shrugging apologetically is punctuated by the statement, "If the gloves don't fit, you must acquit." Perhaps this wasn't the only factor, but it certainly played a role in his shocking acquittal.

So how did a turn of phrase become so powerful? I blame Dr. Seuss. Most of us were exposed to Seuss' whimsical rhymes and colorful characters as children. His nonsensical poems require us to suspend logic and simply enjoy the story. Maybe this conditioned us from our early years to lower our defenses and become less analytical when something rhymes. OK, so maybe I'm just being facetious, but the effects of a clever jingle are undeniable. Bernays believed, "When... the herd must think for itself, it does so by means of clichés, pat words or images which stand for a whole group of ideas or experiences."[1]

"Plop plop, fizz fizz..." One of the most memorable jingles in American culture came about as a campaign to increase sales of Alka-Seltzer. Though all advertisements are designed to increase sales, this one in particular was designed to exactly double the purchases. Initially, most consumers would

1. Bernays, E. L. (2005). Propaganda. New York: Ig Publishing, 74.

take a single tablet of Alka-Seltzer to relieve their suffering, but the jingle itself suggested a doubling of the dose.[2]

Did you know the fun cartoon jingle "Winnie the Pooh and Tigger Too" came from a Presidential election slogan from the 1840s? It was based on a song for Whig candidates William Henry Harrison and John Tyler and was used to mock incumbent Democrat Martin Van Buren. "Tippecanoe and Tyler Too" is better remembered as a slogan than the original song. Harrison was considered a hero from the Battle of Tippecanoe, though his success in this expedition is debatable. Once again, jingles and slogans don't really have to make sense.

Although radio jingles were around in the early 1920's, they became more popular in the late Twenties as a way to get around NBC's restrictions on direct advertising during evening programming. Sponsor's names and product plugs were inserted into the theme songs of many shows like a radio version of

2. Lawrence, M. W. (2003). A Big Life (in Advertising). New York: Touchstone.

product placement.[3] Since then, jingles have evolved from complete songs to just a line or two with a catchy hook, but their influence has only grown.

Slogans also have a unique power in their simplicity. For example, one of the most successful advertising campaigns in history was built around the simple slogan, "A Diamond is Forever." Coined in 1947 by Frances Gerety, in 2000 it was named by Advertising Age magazine the best advertising slogan of the twentieth century.[4]

In 1939, prior to the campaign, ten percent of brides in the U.S. received a diamond engagement ring. By the end of the century, eighty percent of brides were bestowed a diamond ring. Marketing in Japan with the slogan resulted in even more dramatic results. In the 1960s, diamond rings signaled engagement for a mere six percent of brides in Japan. By the beginning

3. McLeod, E. (2005, February). Radio Recall. Retrieved February 27, 2015, from Metropolitan Washington Old Time Radio Club: http://www.mwotrc.com

4. Johnson, D. (2014, August 27). 'A Diamond Is Forever;' How Four Words Changed an Industry. Retrieved November 11, 2015, from Voice of America: http://www.learningenglish.voanews.com

of the 1990's, the number had grown to nearly eighty percent.[5]

According to Gerety, the slogan was simply a last minute thought, scribbled on a slip of paper at the end of a busy day. When later presented at a meeting, it really didn't create much enthusiasm. As Gerety put it, "Nobody jumped." Before long, however, people "jumped" to buy diamonds. The simple, yet effective, slogan was propelled to success by the propagandizing efforts of Dorothy Dignam, another female on the DeBeers marketing team. Although gifted agents behind the success of the engagement ring, ironically, both Frances Gerety and Dorothy Dignam never married.[6]

Edward Bernays often relied on the power of a good slogan to strengthen his message. "By playing upon a[n] old cliché, or manipulating a new one, the propagandist can sometimes swing a whole mass of group emotions." [7]

5. The Global Diamond Industry. (2011). Diamond Industry Report. Bain & Company, Inc.
6. Sullivan, J. C. (2013, May 3). How Diamonds Became Forever. The New York Times.
7. Bernays, E. L. (2005). Propaganda. New York: Ig Publishing, 74.

Consider that the next time you catch yourself whistling a memorable jingle. Just because something sounds good or rolls of the tongue with rhythm, it doesn't mean we should let it slide like a ref at a T-ball game. "Cute" is no excuse for wrong or illogical. "...Empty slogans [are] meant as a substitute for critical thinking. Pretentious jargon [is] designed to lend authority to special interests."[8] Don't fall prey to slogans that are misleading such as "Read my lips, no new taxes" or "If you like your doctor, you can keep your doctor."

Jingles and slogans serve as a great tool against logic or careful evaluation, but propagandists have other techniques to ease our mental objectivity into an effortless autopilot. One method is the narrative. Politically-charged narratives can have tremendous influence over a mass population. As one insightful journalist and writer observes, "A Narrative Watcher would reveal

8. Clark, R. P. (2012, February 20). How "Narrative" Moved from Literature to Politics & What This Means for Covering Candidates. Retrieved October 20, 2015, from Poynter: http://www.poynter.org/2012/how-narrative-moved-from-literature-to-politics-what-this-means-for-covering-candidates/162834/

how political parties and others seeking power use verifiable facts, half-truths, and misinformation to tell stories designed to promote their own interests."[9] A narrative is more than just a story. It is a story with an agenda.

Politicians, in particular, expend great effort to control the narrative. The first Republican debate in 2015 was more an exercise in establishing a personal narrative than a true debate. Many of the 16 candidates seemed to have the same image consultant, drilling into them the value of a humble history. This was probably as a justifiable response to the media pummeling given Mitt Romney in the previous presidential election for being perceived as rich and out-of-touch with the middle class. Although the debates were meant to be extemporaneous, several candidates seemed to work from the same script: "Growing up in _____ (insert rural or middle-class town), I watched

9. Clark, R. P. (2012, February 20). How "Narrative" Moved from Literature to Politics & What This Means for Covering Candidates. Retrieved October 20, 2015, from Poynter: http://www.poynter.org/2012/how-narrative-moved-from-literature-to-politics-what-this-means-for-covering-candidates/162834/

as my father/single mom, a _____ (insert blue-collar job), worked hard to build a better life for his/her children." Marco Rubio even exclaimed, "I was raised paycheck to paycheck!" This attempt at meekness was sometimes followed by a faith-promoting story or scripture to demonstrate their religious credentials. The consistency of this narrative was as awkward as several women showing up at the same party in the same dress.

The award winning British journalist and novelist, John Lanchester notes, "Everybody in politics now seems to talk about narratives all the time; even political spin-doctors describe their job as being 'to craft narratives.' We no longer have debates, we have conflicting narratives. It's hard to know whether this represents an increase in PR sophistication and self-awareness, or a decrease in the general level of discourse."[10]

10. Clark, R. P. (2012, February 20). How "Narrative" Moved from Literature to Politics & What This Means for Covering Candidates. Retrieved October 20, 2015, from Poynter: http://www.poynter.org/2012/how-narrative-moved-from-literature-to-politics-what-this-means-for-covering-candidates/162834/

Watching the sad Michael Brown death/riot/ investigation coverage unfold demonstrates how powerful a narrative can be, in both reporting and consuming the news. The sparseness of facts during the early reporting did not stop many from making Olympic-caliber leaps of logic to establish and keep the narrative intact. It happened on all sides.

Did anyone else notice the disturbing, widespread denial happening through so much of this? Michael Brown was an unarmed teen shot by a white cop. Yes, it's true. So many stopped paying attention right there, selectively eliminating relevant facts that led to the fatal shooting. It's equally true that Michael Brown was an adult who had just robbed a store and been in some kind of scuffle with the police. When facts interfere with a riot-inciting, looting-causing narrative, they must be downplayed, if not ignored. Even Associated Press violated their own stylebook by repeatedly referring to Brown as a "teen" instead of a "man." The latter (the truth) would have violated the narrative and diluted the value of this story.

Within a month of the shooting, if you asked the majority of passively-attentive Americans about Michael Brown they would probably recall he was a poor black kid shot in the back, hands raised, by a racist white cop. It may even evoke the slogan, "Black Lives Matter." The narrative worked like a charm.

We witnessed the same process during the Trayvon Martin shooting. Dead black kid… check. White shooter… check. Presumption of guilt… check. Al Sharpton's plane ticket… purchased. It seems very few observed thoughtfully and patiently to absorb what actually happened.

What is unfortunate is that the truth is blacks are often unfairly targeted, especially in urban areas, and these narrative-driven cases turn out to be destructive in reversing that trend. When it turned out that Trayvon Martin actually smashed the half-Hispanic George Zimmerman's head into the pavement, and the police officer attacked by Michael Brown was defending his own life, many news consumers will likely not take as seriously future legitimate cases of racism.

76

Another current narrative is that the plight of gays is the new civil rights movement. Are gays treated poorly sometimes? Absolutely. But the situation is a vastly different than segregation based on sexual orientation, gay lynchings, separate water fountains, or denied suffrage. There's a problem with poor treatment of gays at some level, but the narrative crafters insist on acceptance of the their extreme version. Anything less is bigotry.

The War on Women is another false storyline. The crux of this particularly insidious narrative is that women are being "denied" birth control. Even the name "War on Women" is so misleading it's laughable. Nobody is blocking any woman from procuring legal birth control. But don't say it, or write it, or broadcast it; it doesn't fit the narrative.

Perhaps the most gallingly inaccurate narrative is that America is a cruel, greedy, intolerant and imperialistic empire. It should come as no surprise that this idea is propagated both internationally and within the United States. America's enemies, and even some envious allies, spread this propaganda like a religion. Here in the U.S., this storyline is pedaled by politicians, Hollywood, and the media. For example, current policy toward immigration (legal and illegal) is among the most welcoming in the entire world.

By contrast, Australia enforces their Migration Reform Act of 1992 with several strict amendments. Authorities are required to detain anyone without a valid visa, including thousands of child refugees seeking asylum. This led Human Rights Watch to react with a repudiating letter to the Prime Minister. France has trampled religious freedom by making it illegal to wear a burqa or headscarf in public because it "interrupts social cohesion." "That many French residents consider face-covering veils an affront to their secular traditions would not provide a legal justification under American laws."[11] Similarly, Switzerland passed a referendum in 2009, voting 57.5% to 42.5%, preventing

11. Ware, L. (2014, July 3). No Headscarves in Schools, No Burqas in Public: Colorblind Racism in France. Retrieved December 16, 2015, from The Huffington Post: http://www.HuffPost.com/us/entry/555732

the construction of Mosque minarets.[12] The same year, Italy passed penalties fining illegal immigrants between €5,000-10,000 and allowing up to six months detention.[13]

Lax enforcement of U.S. immigration policy and establishment of sanctuary cities further represent an overall attitude of mercy and support for those seeking refuge in a better land. The fact that so many people are eagerly seeking U.S. citizenship directly refutes the false narrative. These desperate immigrants know it is a land of great freedom and opportunity with relatively generous programs for the poor and underprivileged. However, truth and logic are easily set aside to promote an agenda. This is particularly an issue with the "fake news" programs, hosted by popular comedians. Once again, wit supplants wisdom. Cleverness is mistaken for truth. Viewers accept the message without critical analysis, partly

12. Stephens, T. (2009, November 29). Minaret Result Seen as 'Turning Point'. Retrieved January 20, 2016, from Swiss Info: http://www.swissinfo.c/eng/
13. Williams, P. (2010, April 29). The World's Worst Immigration Laws. Retrieved December 16, 2015, from Foreign Policy: http://www.foreignpolicy.com/2010/04/29/

because it sounds smart, or at least funny—and wouldn't it be even funnier if it were true?

We are all better off ditching the narratives. Identify and reject them, wherever they originate. Take their power away. Examine. Be thoughtful. Absorb. Then, make a decision independently about what you observe. We will still arrive at different conclusions, of course, but those conclusions will be authentic and honest, as opposed to the spoon-fed conclusions so many are content to lazily accept. From positions of authenticity, the debates will be real and they will be productive -- a far cry from the hollow delusional punditry so common today.

CHAPTER 6: GETTING TO KNOW YOU

"Civilization is the progress toward a society of privacy."
Ayn Rand

Even before Facebook, data mining, computer cookies, and other tools that invade our personal privacy, propagandists understood the importance of knowing their audience. In his book originally published in 1928, Bernays explained the strategy, "His...effort is to analyze his public. He studies the groups which must be reached, and the leaders through whom he may approach these groups."[1] Technology

1. Bernays, E. L. (2005). Propaganda. New York: Ig Publishing, 66.

has only increased the information available to exploit consumer interests. Not only is our every purchase tracked and analyzed, but web sites track how long you spend viewing each page, what links brought you to their page, and what pages lost your interest causing you navigate away from their site. Website analytics has become an entire career branch for marketing. The amount of information collected about us as consumers is growing exponentially, making privacy only an illusion.

A friend recently complained to me she was concerned the department stores knew her child's exact age and birth date, based on coupons mailed to her for diapers and formula, then later training pants and toys, followed years later by school supplies. On the month of the child's birthday, a coupon from the toy store had arrived on schedule since year one. It reminded me of a similar story from an article in Forbes.

The story goes that an angry father chewed out a manager at Target because his teenage daughter was getting coupons in the mail for baby clothes and cribs. "Are you trying to encourage her to get pregnant?" he ranted. Of course, the manager didn't have a clue what the man was talking about and apologized profusely. A few days later, the man had a heart-to-heart with his daughter and found out she was due in August. An interview with one of Target's statisticians, Andrew Pole, revealed that clues are acquired from customer purchases that allow for fairly accurate personalization of marketing. For example, department stores can not only identify when you are expecting, but elucidate the gender of the baby based on the color of the curtains or blankets you purchase.[2] Knowing the level of information collected about each customer makes Target's reported data breech a little more worrisome.

Unfortunately, it doesn't stop at the check-out. Companies collect data (theoretically stripped of identifying information) from the electronic health record at your doctor's office and pharmacy. We all know our phone

2. Hill, K. (2012, February 16). How Target Figured Out a Teen Girl Was Pregnant Before Her Father Did. Forbes.

conversations, emails and texts are not private either. Travel related web sites use cookies to track searches and increase the price when you return to the site to book your ticket. They can also set a different price, depending on whether you search for fares from a PC or Apple device. There is even a marketing term for it this concept. It is called "dynamic pricing."[3]

Before you demand privacy and express outrage about how your habits and personal information are bought and sold to marketers, consider how much information you freely give away on Facebook, Pintrist, or Twitter. "The modern propagandist studies systematically and objectively the material with which he is working in the spirit of the laboratory."[4] Know that everything you post, like, or even view on the web creates an online profile to be studied, tracked, and sold.

Even when we are away from our computers, we are being monitored and studied for

3. Weiss, R. M., & Mehrotra, A. K. (2001). Online Dynamic Pricing: Efficiency, Equity, and the Future of E-commerce. Virginia Journal of Law and Technology , 6 (11).
4. Bernays, E. L. (2005). Propaganda. New York: Ig Publishing, 72.

marketing purposes. There are programs that connect to in-store cameras to record and analyze the path you take as you shop. Some systems even evaluate where your eyes scan and how much time you spend in an area. Using this data, supermarkets can design their store layout down to the location of a product on the shelf. The objective for marketers is to influence your spending habits and manipulate your choices as a consumer to maximize their profits.

Imagine how angry a movie star or famous athlete would be if they discovered their personal assistant (the one booking all their appointments, tracking their spending, and overhearing their personal conversations) was selling their secrets to the tabloids. That person would be justifiably fired on the spot. Now consider that each of us, though likely not rich or famous, employs a personal assistant in the form of a smartphone. We enter appointments, track our spending, text our friends, store our photo albums, and carry on many of our private conversations with the aid of this device. Many people even use apps to track their eating and exercise habits as part of a weight loss regimen. Others monitor menstrual cycles to time intimacy (these apps even recommend you record the day you may have conceived). What happens to this data when your phone is lost, stolen, or hacked?

Don't be lulled by your own sense of obscurity, either. Just because you are not famous or wealthy, it doesn't mean you aren't a target. Identity theft is a growing crime and not particularly selective in its victim. Not only that, but even local police departments have equipment that mimics a cell tower, tricking your phone into connecting and allowing access to your smartphone without a warrant. Certainly criminals also have access to this equipment and the motivation to use it against you, whether for blackmail or fraud. The retailers and marketers don't even need to hack your phone to get access. Many user agreements for the apps you regularly use include allowing access to your personal data.

As in illustration, consider this scenario: You receive a fitness tracker for Christmas and begin wearing it on your wrist, intent on developing healthy habits as a New Year's resolution. This tracker records your sleep and exercise and connects to a program on your smartphone where you enter data about the foods you eat. As you wear this tracker, it also records your movements by GPS and notes that you pass an organic food store and a fitness center on your way to work each day. It also records that it takes you an average of 25 minutes to fall asleep each night.

The next time you sync the wristband to your phone for an update, it sends the map of your movements back to the company that developed the fitness tracker. This information is then sold to a marketing firm for analysis. Within minutes you receive targeted advertising, based on this data. In your email you find a coupon for 20% off a gym membership (the one on your way to work), a rebate for a gallon of organic milk, and an advertisement for a sleep aid medication. A week later, you receive a flyer in the mail for a sale at the runner's outlet. Given your focus on healthy lifestyle changes, you don't even notice this "coincidence" and end up locked into a 1-year gym membership and dependent on sleeping pills that you wash down with organic milk. It's ok, though, because you have two new pairs of stylish sneakers (they were buy one, get the second one ½ price).

CHAPTER 7: PROPAGANDA IN POLITICS AND EDUCATION

"...lack of transparency is a huge political advantage. And basically, call it the stupidity of the American voter or whatever, but basically that was really, really critical to get [Obamacare] to pass."
Jonathan Gruber, Obamacare advisor

With outspoken and controversial characters like Jonathan Gruber leading the way, you can almost smell the arrogance of many of our political leaders today. Their philosophies can be summed up with a quote from our good friend, Edward Bernays, "The conscious and intelligent manipulation of the organized habits and opinions of the masses is an important element in democratic society. Those who manipulate this unseen mechanism of society constitute an invisible government which is the true ruling power of our country."[1] Based on this false and evil premise, they justify their lies and manipulations with the idea that they know better than the average person what is right and good. Their sense of superiority underestimates the intelligence and integrity of the American public. They seem to have forgotten that politicians are meant to be civil servants, not dictators.

"The important thing for the statesmen of our age is not so much to know how to please the public, but to know how to sway the public… If a politician is a real leader he will be able, by the skilled use of propaganda, to lead the people, instead of following the people…"[2] How better to perpetuate and expand the manipulation of public opinion than to exploit

1. Bernays, E. L. (2005). Propaganda. New York: Ig Publishing, 37.
2. Bernays, E. L. (2005). Propaganda. New York: Ig Publishing, 119,125.

the compulsory public education system? With mandatory enrollment of all children during their most formative years, it creates a perfect system to program young, malleable minds. It seems a shame that Edward Bernays is not alive today to see the recent changes in the public education system in America. It likely would have brought him great pleasure to see how the liberal left is finally recognizing the value of education as a tool for propaganda.

In his writings, Bernays lamented, "The public is not cognizant of the real value of education, and does not realize that education as a social force is not receiving the kind of attention it has the right to expect in a democracy... The normal school should provide for the training of the educator to make him realize that his is a twofold job: education as a teacher and education as a propagandist."[3] The Common Core Curriculum seems to have addressed this oversight frighteningly well. Finally, the public education system will realize its proper place for programing the minds of America's youth.

3. Bernays, E. L. (2005). Propaganda. New York: Ig Publishing, 135-136.

If you do not have children attending public school, you may believe the changes taking place in the curriculum do not affect you, but you would be woefully wrong. In a democratic society, all you need is a majority, or even a vocal minority, to create a fundamental transformation of our nation and its laws. Once the influences of the educational propaganda machine take hold, the momentum may be unstoppable.

Using federal and state funding (your tax dollars), today's educational system molds young students into passionate progressives. They are indoctrinated with liberal ideas including zealous environmentalism, amorality (there is no right and wrong—just different), and social justice. They learn to comply with rules and regulations, despite how asinine or nonsensical, without question in order to prepare them to willingly put up with all the regulations created by progressives. Once indoctrinated with these concepts, students are then open to accept government regulation (ie. the overreaching EPA), atheism, and socialism. In fact, the rising generation may even think these concepts are their own idea, much like Bernays' propaganda of the music room made people think buying a piano was their own idea.

The two subjects that are most threatening to the success of the progressive curriculum are history and religion. However, it is not enough to just eliminate these subjects altogether. Educators must attach shame and embarrassment to these topics to ensure they are not even mentioned, except in expressions of apology and regret. If history is remembered correctly, the students may see the error of socialism, for example, reflected in the fate of the U.S.S.R. or Nazi Germany. If religion is properly regarded, the power of the government is displaced by a higher being. Students may recognize their rights and liberties derive from God, rather than their political leaders. The best protection against these threats is for the curriculum to limit its scope of these subjects to shameful topics like slavery and the Inquisition.

This may sound like an extreme perspective of the public school curriculum, but consider this. I was recently speaking with a friend about her

5th grade daughter. She was distressed to learn her child was assigned to read a book about an 11-year old struggling with gender identity and sexual orientation issues. When she demanded to opt her child out of the assigned reading, the offered alternative was a book about an adolescent contemplating suicide. Find out what books are on your district's required reading lists and see for yourself. Review the Common Core Curriculum and think about the agenda it promotes and whom the propaganda is serving.

Another parent mentioned to me his experience when registering a child for school. Some of the questions about demographics were disturbingly inquisitive. For unknown reasons, the district felt it necessary to identify from where they had moved, if anyone in the household worked in agriculture, household income, if any parents had experienced job loss in the last 2 years, etc. When he asked why the information was necessary, the administrators simply shrugged or passed it off as a requirement for the school lunch program. It seems federal funding for this program is linked to compliance with this required data-collection.

It may be that the Department of Education is the propaganda branch of the U.S. government, ensuring a permanent progressive base for generations to come. Perhaps that is what Bernays envisioned when he recommended, "The United States Government should create a Secretary of Public Relations [his euphemism for propaganda] as a member of the President's Cabinet."[4] Or perhaps this job belongs to the "Ebola Czar."

In addition to the education system, political leaders have also tapped into another method of public manipulation. While the movie industry was still in it's infancy, Bernays' recognized the power of Hollywood as a tool for propaganda. In his book publish in 1928 he states, "The American motion picture is the greatest unconscious carrier of propaganda in the world today. It is a great distributor for ideas and opinions." Since that time, Hollywood's influence has only grown. From liberal philosophies

---

4. Bernays, E. L. (2005). Propaganda. New York: Ig Publishing, 127.

written brazenly into scripts to more subtle partisan adjustments in a scene, Hollywood works full-time to promote a political agenda.

For example, when the movie E.T. the Extra-Terrestrial was re-released for it's 20th anniversary, the computer-generated revisions were more than just cosmetic. In a scene where federal agents have set up a roadblock to capture E.T. and Elliot as they escape, the agents' guns were digitally replaced with walkie-talkies. Although it may seem like a minor change, the symbolism is interesting. As the federal government becomes more powerful and more threatening in the real world, Hollywood portrays the federal agents as less pernicious and less dangerous.

Hollywood's role as a shill for politicians is not new. When Calvin Coolidge needed help with his image as a dull, serious man, his image consultant arrange for him to have breakfast with a group of movie stars. He then ensured press coverage complete with photographers. One headline quipped, "Actor Eats Cake with the Coolidges... President Nearly Laughs."[5] As you may have guessed, Coolidge's PR man pulling the strings for this event was none other than Edward Bernays. Based on comments in a 1981 address to the Publicity Club of Chicago, he likely imagined himself among the great patriots when arranging this event. "[American revolutionary leaders] used oratory, newspaper exposure, meetings, or correspondence to rally public opinion to their cause, and as a matter of fact, historical research indicates that Thomas Jefferson wrote the Declaration of Independence as a public relations pronouncement."[6]

Politicians and activists also are gifted at spinning current events into useful propaganda. Recall the media storm when Matthew Shepard, a young gay student, was found brutally beaten and left for dead on a remote highway in Wyoming. Tragically, he died from

---

5. Warming Up Calvin Coolidge. (n.d.). Retrieved December 11, 2015, from The Museum of Public Relations: http://www.PRMuseum.com
6. Bernays, E. (1981, May 15). Public Relations: Yesterday, Today, and Tomorrow. Publicity Club of Chicago, Chicago.

his injuries after being transferred to a hospital in Colorado. Immediately the press focused on his sexual orientation as the motive for the violent murder. His mother became an activist for LGBT rights and on October 28, 2009, President Barack Obama signed the Matthew Shepard Act into law. The new law expanded the definition of hate crimes to include crimes motivated by a victim's gender, sexual orientation, gender identity, or disability.[7]

The problem is, Shepard's sexual orientation was likely not a major factor in his murder. Evidence suggests it was primarily a drug-related robbery that turned fatally violent. Shepard's attackers, the prosecutor, and a lead investigator in the case have made statements to support robbery as the motive, rather than the victim's sexuality.[8] The theory of a hate crime motivation likely arose when Shepard's

7. Riha, A. M. (2009, October 28). President Obama Signs Hate Crime Prevention Act. Retrieved December 14, 2015, from Fox News: http://www.foxnews.com/politics/10/28/
8. ABC News. (2004, November 26). Retrieved December 11, 2015, from New Details Emerge in Matthew Shepard Murder: http://www.abcnews.go.com/2020/story?id=277685&pages=1

friends, Walt Boulden and Alex Trout began contacting the media in the aftermath of the attack claiming the assault occurred because the victim was gay. A close friend of Shepard, Tina Labrie, has since said, "[Boulden and Trout] wanted to make [Matt] a poster child or something for their cause."[9] From there, the spark was kindled and LGBT activists, the media, and politicians ran with the story. We see similar spin by gun control advocates occur in the wake of tragic school shootings. In the words of Rahm Emanuel in discussing government expansion, "You never want a serious crisis to go to waste… This crisis provides the opportunity for us to do things that you could not before."[10]

9. Jimenez, S. (2013). The Book of Matt: Hidden Truths About the Murder of Matthew Shepard. Steerforth.
10. Emanuel, R. (2008, November 19). The Wall Street Journal.

CHAPTER 8:
MARKETING YOU

"Think about what people are doing on Facebook today. They're keeping up with their friends and family, but they're also building an image and identity for themselves, which in a sense is their brand."

Mark Zuckerberg

Although the word "propaganda" has become a dirty word, it would be a mistake to not recognize the advantages of good marketing in our own endeavors. It can be used to promote a positive, truthful message as easily as a negative or deceitful one. In fact, this is sometimes where politicians (particularly those on the right) fail in delivering their message. They rely on the plain and simple truth to promote its self. Because the truth has no agenda, truth speakers often fail to recognize the valuable role of propaganda. Sometimes presentation of the truth in a clear, appealing, or memorable way promotes greater success.

George Creel, director of the U.S. Office of War information, was assigned by Woodrow Wilson the job of marketing World War I to the American public. Given that propaganda was associated with the techniques of America's German enemies, he avoided this term. "Our effort was educational and informative throughout, for we had such confidence in our case as to feel that no other argument was needed than the simple, straightforward presentation of facts."[1] It is unclear if he truly failed to see the advantages of using propaganda, believing the truth needed no garnishment, or simply preferred a different label for propaganda.

1. Creel, G. (1920). How We Advertised America. New York: Harper & Brothers.

One common mistake of promoters (whether politicians, or simply one person trying to convince another) is to rely exclusively on cold, hard facts. Data and statistics are of some value, but often an illustrative anecdote or image is more powerful. For example, over 2,600 Syrian refugees had already died attempting to cross the Mediterranean between January and September 2015. However, it was the haunting image of the body of 3-year-old Aylan Kurdi washed ashore that served as a shocking call to action for people across the globe.[2] It shifted national policies, motivated billionaire philanthropists, and stirred sentiment from even the most detached witnesses.[3]

Emotional or touching experiences draw allegiance from the audience in ways that bare numbers and raw facts cannot. The heart will often lead us where the mind is reluctant to

2. Clarke, R., & Shoichet, C. E. (2015, September 3). Image of 3-year-old Who Washed Ashore Underscores Europe's Refugee Crisis. Retrieved September 6, 2015, from CNN: http://www.cnn.com/2015/09/02/europe/migration-crisis-boy-washed-ashore-in-turkey/
3. Sawiris, N. (2015, September 11). GPS. (F. Zakaria, Interviewer) CNN.

travel. Empathy, in particular, is a powerful motivator. It keys into a very natural and basic part of humanity akin to self-preservation. Almost reflexively, it triggers a sense of, "that could be me or someone I love."

The younger generation seems particularly self-obsessed, making empathy almost necessary to draw a response. The more someone identifies with a cause, the more passionate they become. Humans have a natural tendency to protect and defend those things they consider their own, whether a person, an object, or a cause. It is outside our natural programming as humans to concern ourselves deeply with a vague, statistical group of people we do not relate to or see as our own. A generation absorbed with their autobiographical blog called Facebook, selfies, YouTube, and i_____ brand products will have little energy or interest in things they don't "like." Conversely, if you can convince someone to "like" you or your cause, you tap into a deeper level of devotion.

It should come as no surprise, then, that some people are now increasingly drawn to fame as a primary goal in life. In a Pew Research Survey done in 2006, 51% of those age 18-25 listed "to become famous" as their first or second most important goal in life.[4] Fame creates "friends" where deep, meaningful friendships are lacking. In fact, fame has become a new currency in today's world of constant self-marketing. You can even buy "friends" to boost your numbers in the social media realms, though Twitter and others officially frown on this practice.

There is even a website that will score your influence or fame, based on a complex formula of social media connections, followers, and friends. Publishers have been known to research a writer's clout score as a critical factor in choosing to publish their book with the idea that this will influence its success and promotion. Many actors and athletes are even paid for mentioning products, name-dropping hotels and restaurants, and posting pictures of themselves

4.Kohut, A., Parker, K., Keeter, S., Doherty, C., & Dimock, M. (2007). How Young People View Their Lives, Futures, and Politics: A Potrait of 'Generation Next'. The Pew Research Center for the People & the Press. The Pew Research Center fot the People & the Press.

with recognizable brands. The more friends and followers you have, the higher the paycheck.

Fame has become so venerated that many will even settle for infamy. In 1998, the Secret Service published a psychological case review of 83 individuals who attacked or threatened a public figure. This study found the goal of achieving notoriety as the most common motive behind the attacks.[5] In the 1990s and 2000s it seemed to be school shootings, then it shifted to movie-theatre shootings following a well-publicized massacre in a Colorado theatre. There has even been a suspicious run of "accidentally released" porn tapes that propelled several reality stars' careers.

This dangerously misguided grasp for attention becomes an increasing problem when a terrible act consumes the media spotlight for a period of time. Often, this results in copy-cats also seeking publicity. Evidence of this can be found in the revealing blog linked

5. Fein, R. A., & Vossekuil, B. (1998). Protective Intelligence and Threat Assessment Investigations: A Guide for State and Local Law Enforcement Officials. National Institute of Justice, U.S. Department of Justice. Office of Justice Programs.

to a cowardly school shooter. In it, he eerily describes the results of another intensely publicized double-murder that occurred on live TV weeks before he went on his own killing rampage. The previous event he refers to was also captured by a body cam worn by the killer, then posted to Facebook (more evidence of a desire for public attention). The blog states, "I have noticed that so many people like him are all alone and unknown, yet when they spill a little blood, the whole world knows who they are. A man who was known by no one, is now known by everyone. His face splashed across every screen, his name across the lips of every person on the planet, all in the course of one day. Seems the more people you kill, the more you're in the limelight."[6]

****

Whether we think about it or not, we are continuously presenting an image of ourselves to those around us. Simply stated, propaganda

6. Sider, S., lah, K., Almasy, S., & Ellis, R. (2015, October 2). Victim Tells Dad: Gunman Singled Out Christians. Retrieved November 6, 2015, from CNN: http://www.cnn.com/2015/10/02/us/

happens. Some people, however, choose to focus primarily on image, while often neglecting character. These people will pursue status over personal substance. They are much like the Food Stylists that create mouth-watering images of food for magazines, packaging, signage, movies, and advertisements using some very clever tricks.

For example, since pancakes with maple syrup don't look very good after the syrup has soaked in and the pancakes are soggy, they spray the pancakes with stain repellant (usually used for fabric and upholstery) and replace syrup with motor oil. Another common trick is to stuff paper towels into food items, like sandwiches and burgers, to prop them up and help them hold shape. They apply lipstick to food, giving it the right shade of pink and use eyeliner for brown or black. Since the color of milk doesn't photograph well, they sometimes substitute white glue.[7] The deceptions are endless.

---

7. Zhang, M. (2010, October 14). Secrets of Food Styling and Photography. Retrieved December 2, 2015, from Petapixel: http://www.petapixel.com/2010/10/14/

Imagine what it would be like to bite into one of those tempting meals from the photo shoot. You would likely be disgusted and disappointed. The same response is common when people find out that someone is not as they seem.

CHAPTER 9: LIVING IN SPIN

"Trust no one."
Agent Fox Mulder, The X-Files

So what happens when the public becomes hyperconscious of the ubiquitous nature of propaganda? Few things create stronger resentment than feeling manipulated, and it doesn't take long for skepticism to become paranoia. Just like in the story "The Boy Who Cried Wolf," when people recognize they have been duped they respond with distrust and sometimes anger. This response is intensified when the manipulation is done with malice or conceit. Independence and free-thinking are fundamental to American culture so it is nature to rebel against those that attempt control through manipulation.

The result is increasing mistrust toward government and scientists. A recent article in the New England Journal of Medicine (NEJM) referenced a November 2014 poll by Quinnipiac University that found, "only 14% of the public said they trusted the federal government to do what is right 'almost all the time' or 'most of the time,' which is one of the lowest proportions since researchers began tracking this measure in 1958." This interesting article explored the implications of public perception (and perhaps misperception) relating to Ebola. "Although there had been only two cases of Ebola transmission inside the United States and both patients survived, a November 2014 opinion poll revealed that the U.S. public ranked Ebola as the third-most-urgent health problem facing the country…" [ranking it] "…higher than any other disease, including cancer or heart disease, which together account for nearly half of all U.S. deaths each year."[1]

1. SteelFisher, G. K., Blendon, R. J., & Lasala-Blanco, N. (2015). Ebola in the United States -- Public Reactions and Implications. New England Journal of Medicine , 373 (9), 789-791.

The article goes on to explore possible reasons for this apparently irrational response to a perceived crisis.

One obvious explanation was that the media likely affected public perception, creating an exaggerated sense of danger from Ebola. In a period of just a few weeks, the nightly news programs of three major networks aired over 1000 segments about Ebola. The article also explained that the style of coverage likely affected public perception. By naming the individual patients that contracted the disease in the U.S. (there were only two) and following their stories, public concern was dramatically increased. This same phenomenon occurs with animals and has been repeatedly demonstrated in studies of behavioral psychology.

For example, consider the worldwide outrage when a dentist was led on a "canned hunt" in Zimbabwe and ended up killing a lion named Cecil. The anger and contempt lasted for weeks and even overshadowed another truly despicable exposure of human depravity (Horrific videos of living babies being dissected after abortion and sold for parts had just been released). The mass outrage over Cecil the Lion seems completely irrational when viewed in context.

To begin with, according to a Zimbabwean newspaper, "It is not an overstatement that almost 99.99 percent of Zimbabweans didn't know about this animal until Monday. Now we have just learnt, thanks to the British media, that we had Africa's most famous lion all along, an icon!"[2] Despite the international response, his home country was nonplussed.[3] Secondly, trophy hunts are not uncommon. According to Adams Roberts, CEO of the animal rights group "Born Free USA," more than 500 lions are killed every year in Africa as trophies.[4] It really doesn't make sense that this one hunt stood out from hundreds of others.

2. Mavhumashava, K. (2015, July 30). Cecil: What's Going On? The Chronicle.

3. Dzirutwe, M. (2015, August 5). 'What Lion?' Zimbabweans Ask, Amid Global Cecil Circus. Reuters.

4. Lewis, K., Powell, A., & Kelly, K. J. (2015, October 2). Cecil the Lion Could Help Protect Other Animals. Retrieved October 3, 2015, from VOA News: http://www.learningenglish.voanews.com

Finally, why did the death of a single lion garner so much attention in the overall setting of dramatically declining lion populations? Although the data varies, most estimates reveal that, in the last fifty years, the lion population in Africa has dropped from around 100,000 to about 30,000.[5] It seems that a few tears from late night host and comedian, Jimmy Kimmel, make all the difference. Within 24 hours of his on-air breakdown over Cecil, Oxford's Wildlife Conservation Research Unit (the group responsible for tracking the lion) received $150,000 in donations.[6] With that level of influence, it's no wonder fame is so desired today. The irrationality of Cecil the Lion's story parallels well with the discussion about America's response to Ebola.

Going back to the article from NEJM about Ebola in America, among the reasons postulated for irrationally high levels of public concern,

5. Riggio, J., Jacobson, A., Dollar, L., Bauer, H., Becker, M., Dickman, A., et al. (2012, December 2). The Size of Savannah Africa: a Lion's (Panthera leo) View. Biodiversity and Conservation.
6. Dodds, E. (2015, July 30). Jimmy Kimmel's Cecil the Lion Plea Leads to More Than $150,000 in Donations. Time.

the authors state, "people did not understand, or perhaps did not believe, information about how this gruesome disease spreads." Out of context, statements like this hint of conceit among scientist that they, perhaps, believe the public is too dumb to understand this disease. However, the more critical factor is probably that the public did not believe the information disseminated by scientists at the Centers for Disease Control. Americans have developed a sense of skepticism for both scientists and federal government agencies. One only has to consider the conflicting information from the scientific community regarding global warming to discover why even the scientists are suspect.

The conclusions of the NEJM article are particularly interesting. The authors suggest a possible means of overcoming this skepticism. They propose, "...it may be useful to have preestablished (sic) relationships with independent health professional associations that are trusted by the public in order to come to broad agreement on policies and approaches before they are shared with the public."[7] Once again, the solution is to develop a propaganda machine, relying on the reputations of those perceived as trustworthy.

Although scientists and their claims are often met with scrutiny from the public, the case is even grimmer for the government. Conspiracy theories abound. From the assignation of JFK, the lunar landing, area 51, Obama's birth certificate, the 9/11 attacks, the list is nearly endless. Many of these theories are based on a model of rhetoric called the Hegelian Dialectic. Based on a three-stage formula of logic including thesis, antithesis, and synthesis, it provides a framework on which to build a logical conspiracy plot or storyline.

We can apply this formula to examine how the current issue of global warming evolved. The thesis, or conflict, is that the world is warming up due to man-produced CO_2. The antithesis, or solution, is to create hysteria and fear using the media to impart emotional involvement.

7. SteelFisher, G. K., Blendon, R. J., & Lasala-Blanco, N. (2015). Ebola in the United States -- Public Reactions and Implications. New England Journal of Medicine , 373 (9), 789-791.

Finally, the synthesis, or resolution is to use high emotion to implement global regulation that would otherwise be politically impossible. A cunning or manipulative leader can even use this pattern to create conflict or crisis that demands a resolution, allowing those orchestrating the crisis to swoop in with a ready-made solution that otherwise may not be approved.

Some people have speculated that the true purpose of Obamacare was to deepen the healthcare crisis with bad policy and intentionally collapse the healthcare system. In the resulting chaos and desperation, leaders could promote a single-payer system as the solution. Prior to the crisis, a proposal of a nationalized healthcare program would have been met with a resounding "NO!" After cycling through the conflict, it becomes a viable resolution. Anyone challenging this as merely a cynical conspiracy theory hasn't been reading the headlines.

Bernie Sanders, a self-proclaimed Socialist, has made the single-payer system (read "government run") his mantra. From his days as a mayor of a college-town in Vermont to his rise in the polls as a presidential candidate, this platform has evolved from quixotic to brilliant, at least for Progressives. Following a tall glass of Kool-Aid, Vermont physician Dr. Deb Richter proclaims, "Obamacare was hyped as this savior, and it has not been that." Sander's supporters feel the so-called Affordable Care Act has not done enough.[7] They are now reaping the harvest of a well-cultivated conflict as it emerges from a season of Hegelian dialectic.

Ironically, a politician especially gifted at propaganda can manipulate the public by feeding their suspicions and conspiracy theories. How better to mislead than to create the illusion that you are revealing treachery. Given that the public is seeking intrigue, it may be wise to begin pointing the finger at others before you become a suspect. Such political spin, and the ensuing public suspicion, is nothing new.

According to legend, in 1787 Empress Catherine II of Russia set out on tour of the newly annexed territory of Southern Ukraine and Crimea. The area had suffered famine and destruction following years of war, but Grigory Potemkin, governor of the region now called "New Russia" was eager to showcase his progress in development and repair. An ambitious man, he had built a key naval port on the Black Sea, implemented farming projects, built fortresses, and establish several towns.

Intending to impress her allies, Catherine brought her court of European diplomats on the six-month cruise down the Dnieper River. As Catherine's good friend and former lover, Potemkin went above and beyond to amaze. He arranged for displays of rockets and sharpshooters. He even had entire villages constructed of pasteboard and imported herds, flocks, and thousands of peasants from surrounding areas to populate the banks of the river. Each night, the mock villages were taken down and moved farther downstream as the Empress continued her voyage.

The irony of this legend is that Grigory Potemkin is accused of perpetuating propaganda when he was more likely was a victim of propaganda. Historians now believe "Potemkin villages," which today are synonymous with a sham or fraud, were not as phony as the legend purports. The evidence suggests, although Potemkin led a campaign to tidy up and decorate the villages along the banks of the river, entire towns were not manufactured. Beggars were banished from view, facades were created to hide dilapidated buildings, and villagers were encouraged to appear industrious, but it was not the full charade perpetuated by myth. The widespread acceptance of this fable today is supported, in part, by the ease of finding a modern correlation. We frequently hear of Olympic villages that are actually Potemkin villages during their bid to host the games[8][9] and even the liberal state of Hawaii has been known to provide one-way tickets its homeless before tourist season.[10]

8. Farber, M. (2014, February 6). Sochi's Winter Olympics Nothing More Than a 21st Century Potemkin Village. Sports Illustrated.

9. Waxman, O. B. (2013, July 31). Hawaii Offers Homeless One-Way Tickets Out of State. Time.

10. Covert, B. (2014, November 3). To Clear Waikiki for Tourists, Hawaii Gives 120 Homeless People a One-Way Ticket Out of State. Retrieved November 4, 2015, from Think Progress: http://www.thinkprogress.org/economy/2014/11/03/3587685/

The phrase "Potemkin villages" is attributed to Georg von Helbig, Saxon envoy to Catherine's court. Although he was not present on the tour of Crimea, he spread the rumors and exaggerations, and even included the story in a biography of Grigory Potemkin written years after Potemkin's death so it could not be contended.[11] When politicians spread propaganda accusing an adversary of creating propaganda, the spin upon spin is dizzying.

Walking the fine line between healthy skepticism and paranoia can be challenging. Those who claim a conspiracy behind every event or issue weaken their arguments on legitimate scandals. To borrow again from childhood stories, they become like Chicken Little who ran around shouting, "The sky is falling! The sky is falling!" Maintaining this balance requires thoughtful effort, wisdom, and, sometimes, inspiration.

---

11. Adams, C. (2003, November 14). Did 'Potemkin Villages' Really Exist? Retrieved January 20, 2016, from The Straight Dope: http://www.straightdope.com/columns/read/2479/